“Let’s calm things down”

“Let’s calm things down”

By

Alexis Robertson Udip CTBM PPDTI, Adv

Author: Alexis Robertson
Coverdesign: Caroline Miller/Alexis Robertson
ISBN: 9789403624525

Index:

"I would like to dedicate this book to my assistant trainers and very good friends Bina, Claire and Sue. Three ladies who have supported me and encouraged me to write this.
Here they are with Linda and Annie at Crufts where my club was doing a demonstration

To Sandra, from Ashford Dog Training Club, for helping me on my dog training path and finally to my inspirations, my biggest teachers, my dogs Jazz, Charlie, Mavis and Alfie, all four gone but never forgotten".

Who is this book for......?

It is dedicated to those owners who are looking for a way to turn their stressful walks with their anxious companion into something for the partnership to enjoy. For those people who wish to build their dogs' confidence and decrease their anxiety around other dogs. I know how difficult and stressful it can be to have an anxious dog, to feel helpless and deflated when you arrive home after a difficult walk. Often, we are embarrassed at not knowing what to do, other owners looking at us in disgust and we are left apologising whenever another dog appears on our walks. Working in rescue, I see it all too often, and this book has the sole purpose of giving another option for people to consider, to help their dog.

In my opinion we owe our dogs the chance to make better choices, to learn to listen to us so that we can show them we have their backs and to keep them safe. If you follow this book, you will be giving your dog a chance to change your walks for good.

I do want to note that although similar methods can work with human aggression, my advice would be to seek professional help from a recommended behaviourist/trainer in person to ensure you keep your dog and other people safe. Equally, if you feel your dog is putting yourself in danger due to redirected aggression (where he/she will turn on you in frustration), please seek help in person from a reputable trainer.

Introduction:

I remember the day that I realised that my walks may not be as I had imagined them, casually strolling with other people and their dogs and making friends on the way.

My girl Jazz had just turned six months old and until that point she had been friendly and had seemed happy to meet other people and dogs on walks, but something had changed, she seemed fearful, she started barking at every dog! She was a German Shepherd that I had had, since eight weeks old, I had been going to classes and, in fact, still was, but as she hit adolescence her fear came to the forefront. Had I missed the signs? Absolutely, this was nearly 20 years ago, before I had even thought of following my dog training dreams or studying dogs at all.

I immediately sought some help from a professional called Sandra, she was my instructor at the classes and she taught me a lot about how my dog was feeling, how I could help my dog and the changes that I would need to put in place.....you see I also had another GSD and so my walks needed to change to walking Jazz individually so that she could be my main focus.
And so, my journey began, one that I would not have missed for the world. A journey that sent me on my learning path, a journey that has enabled me to help

many others with their overreactive, fearful dogs.

From 2005 I began my learning journey. I did a canine behaviour and management level 5 university diploma, attended many courses, seminars and read what feels like a million books! I was lucky enough to start working with dogs, enabling me to observe their behaviour for myself. I set up my own dog walking business and training classes; this really enabled me to observe dog's behaviour, helping me learn every day.

Now I am the animal welfare manager at an animal rescue; for me, my dream job. We pride ourselves on taking in 'difficult' dogs and giving them their chance of a future.

As for Jazz, she sadly left me in 2014 at the age of 12, but the day before she passed, she had enjoyed a walk with five of her canine friends. I will forever be grateful to have had her in my life.

Chapter 1: Let's calm things down

My aim in this book is to help as many dogs and, of course, their people that I can, to start their journey to enjoyable walks, to create a stronger relationship between human and dog and to ensure less dogs end up in rescue. I hope to do this without too much jargon or science. I want this book to be easy to follow for everyone, a book where you don't have to know much about dogs but, by the end, you've managed to improve your dog's life. This book is about focusing on building the relationship with your dog, not your lead or any other tool, but your dog. A dog that listens, trusts you and a dog that can feel better about his/her walks.

If this book can help a few dogs stay out of rescue and stay within the family that they have learned to love, then it has done its job.

There are many reasons that a dog may be anxious, let's just look at some of these reasons as it may help you understand your dog.

Genetics – If a nervous dog is bred from, this can be passed down to some or all of the litter, meaning they are much more likely to be nervous by nature. This is why breeding is something that should be done by those who know exactly what they are doing both health wise but, just as importantly, behaviour wise.

Lack of Socialisation – The early weeks and months for a puppy are very important, a time to learn and build confidence around 'life', from sights, sounds, people and of course dogs. When a puppy is not exposed in a pleasant way to these things it can cause anxiety as the puppy develops.

Trauma – If a dog or puppy is exposed to a traumatic experience such as an attack from another dog, this can have a detrimental effect on his/her future encounters with other dogs.

Breeds – Some breeds have traits that mean they have a natural suspicion of other dogs or animals. For these breeds dog on dog socialisation and exposure needs to be done from a very early age, the breeder should be able to advise or seek the help of a trainer.

Pain – If your dog's reactivity has started suddenly, or any behaviour change has been noted recently, a vet check would be advised. A dog's behaviour can be connected to pain/discomfort and it is important to rule this out before starting training.

These are just some of the reasons you may now have an anxious overreactive dog, most likely a dog who has now successfully learnt that if they bark and lunge at other dogs, they will in fact go away! Practising this behaviour means your dog can become more successful and confident in his/her manner when out, but likely still feels anxious under their loud façade.

One of the first things I would like you to consider is your dog's current state. Let me explain what I mean! When a dog overreacts due to fear, their adrenaline levels soar very quickly but the decrease in levels takes a lot longer. In the dog world we call this trigger stacking. Basically, with dogs usually getting two walks a day, imagine every walk they may see several dogs, each time their fear rears its ugly head and their adrenaline goes up and down. The main problem is, they never get long enough to fully come back down to a calm level before they are off out on another walk again. And so, the cycle continues.

If this sounds familiar, then the first thing I would suggest you do is give your dog a week off walks........ I heard you gasp! Seriously, a week without walks will allow your dog to relax and, let's be honest, you too, but this doesn't mean you get a week off!

The week will be spent improving your relationship by working on play and focus. Dogs can manage without walks so long as we entertain them with play, training and mental stimulation. Something else that can be useful for your overreactive dog is a daily chewing session, no, not your furniture or shoes, but a long lasting natural chew would be ideal. Chewing is said to help release stress but it also gives your dog an activity to help occupy them.

We all too often think “we must walk the dog”. Personally, I have always given my dogs a day off each week where we don’t go out, we just stay home enjoying each other’s company by doing some fun training, playing in the garden or in fact all having a rest! Why would dogs not need to recharge their batteries like we do? The other often heard misconception is that “the more I walk him the more tired he will be”. I disagree with this too. Yes of course dogs need walks, yes they need exercise but they also need to switch off.

Imagine having a high energy breed, such as a working spaniel or working border collie. Your natural feeling may be, the more I exercise him/her, the more relaxed and tired he/she will be and so the better behaved! Nope! The more he/she may expect, the more likely he/she is to not be able to relax and switch off and so what you really end up with is a highly strung, very tired dog who cannot stop.

If we want a calm dog to live with, we need to help create this.

So, please think about starting this process with a week off walks.

A quick note at this point about equipment you may need to follow the training in this book. A treat bag is a must for quick access when needed, a decent lead (I like the training leads with 2 clips), a longline, a muzzle where deemed necessary (we will discuss this later) tuggy toys (not balls), possibly a head collar (we will cover this later too) and most of all your positive attitude that you can do this and a touch of humour, after all if we don't have that what do we have!

Let the training begin.

Chapter 2: Let the training begin

So, with your week off walks you now have plenty of time to start your new training. Your first job is to find out what motivates your dog, would they rather have food, toys or social interaction with you.......sometimes we think we know what our dogs want but it's always worth testing things out to be sure!

Food: When using treats for training I always find that dogs like something extra smelly and tasty. Usually these can be home-made rather than paying lots of money to buy them. I have found the most successful treats are cheese, sausages or cooked chicken in garlic! There are several recipes out there for tuna cake or salmon cake.

Toys: When I think of playing with my dogs, I think of a mutual game where we are both involved, I don't think of fetch. So, for me the best toys are the long fluffy types that you and your dog can hold at the same time. This toy should only be brought out when you want to play or reward your dog, it's not a toy that the dog can access at any time. Later you will see what I call 'rules of play', in my opinion every game needs some rules and controlling play helps with improving your dog’s impulses.

Affection: To some dogs the verbal praise and physical affection they get from their owner is something they crave, something that brings them pure joy. To some dogs however, this is not something they enjoy. It is simple to see, if your dog leans into you and asks for more when you stop then it is likely that you have a dog who loves it. If, however, your dog moves away, looks uncomfortable or even cowers at too much enthusiasm then this of course cannot be a reward. A reward is only ever something we enjoy, that is true of everyone and every dog. So please look to see how your dog reacts to enthusiastic praise and touch before deciding this is their reward.

Before we start working with the dog, I'd like you to think of your 'marker' word, this is a simple word that lets your dog know when he/she gets something right. The marker word is going to be very important for all the training within this book so choose something that suits you, something you will easily say. Personally, I prefer to use the word 'yes', it's short, easy and positive. The marker word is used when your dog does the behaviour you were looking for and is initially followed by a reward.

So, it may go something like this “Sit”, dog sits and you say “yes” followed by a treat or play or big fuss! Simple! It helps the dog to know what's right without us humans chatting away to them, dogs learn better with clear and easy instruction.

So, choose your word and let's get training.

Whilst at home this week you are going to work on your basic obedience, bringing it to a higher level if you've already done some or getting started if you're new to it.

But you also need to increase your bond with your dog, to be able to focus on you when out and about. You will need a dog that 'wants' to listen to you, that trusts you and knows you have his back!

Play

Like humans, dogs enjoy playing but also like us, there is a need for some control and rules, after all if there were no rules in football it would probably end up a bloody mess!!
So, your first job is to learn to play with your dog with toys and food. We are going to start with food. Food is easy to manage in play and usually maintains most dogs' focus. You'll need some tiny tasty treats, some space and some enthusiasm! The following games just take a minute or two each and I would encourage you to do them every day at least once and continue to do them when out on walks once you get back out there.

- Attention to name – Get your dog's attention, toss a treat a couple of feet away from you and wait for your dog to eat it, as soon as its eaten, say your dog's name. As soon as your dog turns to look your way say your marker word (I am going to use the word 'yes' throughout the rest of this book) and reward your dog with another treat. Repeat this several times and you should soon start to see quicker responses.

- Extending the attention to name game – The same as above but this time as they respond to their name you make a dash away; you should have the dog rushing to catch you up! The 'yes' comes as soon as they turn their focus to you and don't forget to follow it with a reward.

- Through the legs – Toss the treat out as before, say the dog's name and this time as they turn and you say 'yes', toss the treat between your legs. Repeat this several times.

- Round the owner – Again same as before but this time as the dog turns towards you, lure them around your body and toss the treat out. Remember to say 'yes' when your dog turns his/her focus to you.

Not only can these games encourage more focus on you, but they will also make you seem more fun! That is, of course, if you bring out your inner child and really play with them! Your dog needs a play mate, make sure that play mate is you.

Now to bring out the toys! The way I see play is, it's where two participants interact together in a fun activity. So, I would see tuggy as a good game, whereas fetch for me has minimal interaction. First thing to do is find the right toy, a toy that your dog wants to grab and a toy long enough for both your hand and his mouth. I prefer the long soft tuggy toys myself but clients often say that their dog will destroy it, well, my answer to that is that your dog won't get the chance as this toy is for just when the two of you play, it should be put away after play. As I said before, every game needs rules, these are mine:

1. A command like 'take it' should be given, to let the dog know when he is allowed to take hold of the toy.

2. The dog jumps up to snatch the toy before you are ready, lift the toy high up above your head. (This should never be done with dogs known for mouthing, aggression around toys or dogs that lunge at people when over excited) until he stops. Lower it again and repeat until you can hold it at waist height without the dog jumping. Remember, he needs to wait to be asked to play.

3. Don't let go of the toy, this is a game for person and dog, not a chance for him to run off with the toy!

4. Keep the game brief, a few minutes is plenty.

5. The dog needs to give the toy up when asked. Commands like 'drop' or 'give' can be taught. When the dog has the toy in his mouth, offer a treat, as he drops the toy to take the treat, say 'drop'. Eventually the treat won't be needed. If the dog won't let go for a treat, another way is to take the collar and hold it up so the dog cannot lie down or run off and then you let go of the toy and wait for the dog to release the toy.

6. Keep the toy low so as not to encourage jumping.

7. BE EXCITING AND FUN, to believe you are the best game he can have, you have to prove it!

8. Once the game session is over, put the toy away until next time, don't leave it with the dog. This keeps it interesting.

Make sure that playing with food and toys now becomes a part of your day with your dog, it only takes a few minutes at a time and once you are back walking you can easily incorporate this into your walks. After all, dogs really like to have fun and why shouldn’t that be with you.

Now for the training part of this week.

In this first week we are going to work on a few useful commands, leave, look, wait and heel.

The leave will be useful for when you are ready to see dogs again and your dog’s threshold is over its limit (more about that later). It also promotes self-control, something dogs don't naturally have much of!

The look is a great command for keeping eye contact between you and your dog, if your dog can focus on you, he cannot be staring at other dogs!

The wait is a must, teaching impulse control.

The heel and lead walking are often something a nervous overreactive dog is not good at. Being restrained on a lead can make a dog feel more insecure as it removes the 'flight' part of their natural instincts. But to have an overreactive dog out in front of you when walking on lead means that you are already not in control and your dog will feel that he/she must make all their own decisions. As much as this may be hard work for you, it is worth working on. A head collar may be useful for those of you with strong dogs but please ensure you introduce these positively to your dog and seek advice from a trainer if needed.

For the next week start working on the following:

The Leave command:

There are many times when we wish our dogs would stop licking, picking up, eating and rolling in 'stuff' when out on walks. There are also times when we need our dog to stay away from other dogs or people/joggers/bikes/prams....and the list goes on! So, a 'leave' command is a must in my opinion, for every dog. It takes a good few weeks to get a solid 'leave' command, so be patient, put in the work and you'll get the rewards! Only move on through the stages when your dog is spot on with each previous stage.

Stage 1: Teach them the word. With a treat in one hand and another treat readily available to you, open your hand with the treat and have it in the flat of your hand at the dog's face level. As you do this, say 'leave'. Because your dog does not yet understand, he will probably try to take the treat. Close your fingers to prevent this but keep your hand where it is. The dog may sniff/lick/nibble/paw at your hand, ignore all this and say nothing. As soon as your dog gives up for a second, re open your hand repeating the 'leave' command. Repeat as above until you can have the hand open and your dog leaves it for a second, immediately praise and give the other treat from your other hand, then take the other hand away. DO NOT GIVE THE TREAT THAT YOU WERE USING AS A 'LEAVE' OBJECT. We want the dog to understand that 'leave' means it cannot have it AT ALL.

Stage 2: Now that your dog is leaving the food in your hand, you want it to now look away from it and put his attention back on to you. You do this by holding off giving the reward. Do the same as above but this time hold off giving the reward until your dog gives you a second of eye contact, as soon as he does, praise him and give the reward. Timing is important if you want the dog to know which behaviour you wanted.

Stage 3: Now start holding the leave hand lower to the ground, you are building up to putting the food on the floor but do it gradually. Repeat as above. By now your dog should be leaving first time of asking, if not, you have moved on too quickly so go back a stage.

Stage 4: Now place the food on the floor, saying 'leave' as you do so. Because it is no longer in your hand your dog may be more tempted, so keep a hand or your foot nearby just in case. Reward as before.

Stage 5: Now that your dog is good at leaving still objects, you need to work on moving objects. You start this by dropping a piece of food only from a couple of inches off the floor, saying 'leave' as you do so. You can have a lead on at this point to prevent any mishaps! Once your dog is good at this, increase the height inch by inch until you can confidently be standing up, toss a piece of food on the floor and your dog 'leaves' it. TAKE YOUR TIME, SET THE DOG UP TO SUCCEED.

Stage 6: Now instead of just using food, practice with other objects, anything the dog is not allowed ie dinner plate, picture frame, kids toys etc. We need the dog to generalise that 'leave' means 'leave' no matter what you are talking about.
When taking your 'leave' command out and about on walks, which you should now be ready to do, practice your 'leave' with things in the real world whilst your dog is on lead. Eg -: you are walking past some bin bags, as soon as your dog looks at them, say 'leave' and encourage your dog to move away by encouraging him towards you. Reward and praise.

Start by using 'stuff' that your dog is not that bothered about and gradually increase to the things he is more interested in. Never be afraid to move back a stage whenever needed, in order for this command to be solid, your dog must be excellent at each stage before you progress.

To teach a strong leave, it will take several weeks of daily training sessions. They only need to be short sessions but regular sessions will help you progress.

The Heel position:

An important thing to remember about lead walking is that you are walking the dog, this means have a relationship with the dog, not your lead. We tend to rely on the lead being tight to make us feel in control but the point is we want them not to cause a tight lead, so how does that work if we do? Teach the dog what we want them to do and the lead is just there to keep them safe.

1/ Firstly teaching your dog where to be and where the best place to walk is. Choose a side where you want your dog to walk and teach your dog what this position is called ...so either 'heel', 'close' or something that suits you. Remember to only say the word once the dog is in place and then say 'yes' and reward. Practice this several times in each session.

2/ Once you have done the above then start moving a couple of steps ahead and saying 'yes' and reward if the dog stays with you. If the dog walks off ahead...STOP walking and step back, encourage them back to the heel position. Initially you need to do this every few steps, gradually increasing the steps as your dog improves.

Remember not to stoop!! You can still stay upright with the dog knowing you have food.

This seems a good place to mention equipment that may help with those dogs who are very strong and you may be concerned that you struggle to hold them. There are many products out there claiming they are 'no pull', most of which do not have much effect.

There are two pieces of equipment that I sometimes use for particularly strong dogs. One is a front connecting harness made by Perfect Fit; the lead being attached to the chest of the dog can allow for much more control of an overreactive dog.

The other one is a Gencon; this is a head collar that allows much more control. Both of these mean that you can have more control over the front of the dog, the end that is doing the barking and lunging. I have added the links to these items at the back of the book.

The Look:

Getting your dog's attention when out and about is very handy. Not only can it get you past distractions and stop your dog from interfering with other people, but it also helps to lower your dog's desire to go after the distraction, whether it be through excitement, aggression, frustration or fear. Like most training it needs to be started at home and then once your dog has learned the lesson well, you can introduce it out in the real world.

Stage 1: Take a treat and let your dog know you have it, take it up to your eye line and when your dog looks, praise and give the reward. Repeat this several times.

Stage 2: Now in the same way as above but this time add the 'cue', which for this exercise can be 'look' or 'watch' or anything else that suits you. Say the cue as your hand reaches your eye line.

Stage 3: Now have a treat ready in your other hand but use an empty hand to signal to your eyes, say cue word, then praise and reward with your other hand.

Stage 4: Now extend the length of time that your dog needs to hold your gaze before getting the treat. Remember build it up in steps, don't push your dog to fail.

Stage 5: Now practice with your dog in the home, but the dog needs to do it whilst walking a step or two. Remember build up distance gradually and your dog should still be getting a treat every time.

Stage 6: You should now be ready to take the exercise outside in the real world and usually I would expect it to have taken a couple of weeks to reach this stage. When you try this out on walks, do it first when there are no distractions, set your dog up to succeed. Then gradually work on it with more distractions. If your dog has a particular like/dislike of people/dogs/bikes etc, they should be the last thing that you try this command for, so that your dog has had all the training it should need to succeed. Don't stop giving the treat too soon, firstly change the value of the treat to a lower value one, then have a variable ratio of sometimes treats and sometimes a good old fuss and verbal praise.

The look training is simple and just needs to be practiced regularly over a few weeks before introducing it outside on walks but being able to get your dog's focus on you will be very important with your overreactive dog.

When you think of how the reactivity begins, it is with the dog staring at the other dog. Allowing the stare means the dog's adrenalin will surge and their next move is likely to be one that you are trying to prevent. Being able to switch your dog's focus will help keep him/her calmer.

The Wait:

It’s very handy to have a command that your dog understands means you need him to stay still until you tell him to relax or do something else.

Stage 1 - Ask him to sit then hold a treat to his nose and take a step away from him. If he gets up, say 'no' (calmly) and put him/her back where he was and start again. Repeat this until you can step away and he/she doesn't move. When this happens, step straight back to him/her and praise then give the treat. (It’s important to verbally and physically praise a dog calmly as well as give the treat so that he/she doesn't come to rely on the treat).

Stage 2 - Once stage 1 is going really well, where he is not moving off the spot anymore, you can introduce the command. Now have the treat ready but not on his nose, hold the flat of your hand out towards him/her and say 'wait', take the step away. If he/she moves, correct as above, if he/she waits, go back and reward as above. You must take your time getting him/her steady in the 'wait' before you can expect them to do any distance or around any distractions. Don't test your dog, remember you are training so always go at their pace.

Once you have a steady wait, start working on distance and length of time. The final criteria to work on is distraction but first make sure you create a steady wait; the foundations are really important.

The wait also helps teach your dog self-control, after all you can't make a dog wait, he/she has to choose to stay still and this means they are controlling themselves.

One last thing, some of you may feel that your dog could do with is a muzzle, maybe a muzzle would allow you to relax?

One thing we have to get over in this country is that a dog in a muzzle is scary, I mean, where is the sense in that?! Surely a muzzled dog is far safer than an aggressive dog without one? I would also suggest considering muzzle training if a) your dog has previously bitten another dog or b) your dog has a tendency to redirect. Redirected aggression is where your dog's frustration at not being able to 'get to' the other dog means he/she turns on the nearest thing….You! For safety reasons please consider the following muzzle training during this first week.

A basket muzzle is the best choice in my opinion, it allows room for panting, drinking and you can still administer treats.

Start by allowing the dog to examine the muzzle, letting the object become familiar. This may involve you leaving it out for the dog to become accustomed to it.

Next you are going hold the muzzle in the flat of your hand and place some treats inside, ensure you use your hand to cup the muzzle to prevent the treats falling out. Place the treats just inside so the dog only has to touch the muzzle to take the treats. As your dog becomes more comfortable with this, move the treats further down into the muzzle. This allows for your dog to gradually move his/her nose further into the muzzle.

Continue to do this until your dog is comfortable and happy to place his/her nose right into the muzzle and use enough treats that the dog stays inside the muzzle for a few seconds, you can also administer more treats through the muzzle once the dog is comfortably in position.

Your next step is to progress to doing up the muzzle clip and then release it again, keep it brief initially so that you don't unsettle your dog. Spend several sessions doing this. Gradually increase the length of time that the clip is done up, always keep an eye on how your dog feels about it, ideally removing the muzzle before your dog becomes unsettled. You can give treats during the time your dog is wearing the muzzle.

If your dog is comfortable wearing the muzzle then it is not another added stress that your dog does not need!

So, now you have your first week's work to get on with, it would be a good time to put the book down and get started with training. Near the end of the week, move on to the next chapter. Remember, enjoy it, relax (a relaxed and calm owner helps a dog to be the same) and build on your relationship.

Chapter 3: The threshold test

Hopefully you and your dog have had a stress free week and so it's time to move on to the next stage.

This is where we need to find your dog's threshold. What this basically means is, how close can your dog be to another dog before he/she starts to overreact. Every dog will be different, for example, some dogs only get anxious and start barking and lunging when another dog is a few feet away, others only need to spot a dog in the distance and boom, they start! But all of them will have a distance where they have seen a dog but have yet to react badly, this is their threshold.

The reason you need to know what your dog's threshold distance is, is because your initial work needs to start below threshold where you can still get your dog's attention and where your dog has not begun to bark/lunge/growl etc.

It's all well and good us teaching overreactive dogs obedience, that just means they will listen but why wouldn't we want to help make them feel better, feel less threatened, less anxious?

Working with a dog under threshold means they are more relaxed and more open to learning, allowing us a chance to try and change how they feel about seeing other dogs, a window to associate something nice with other dogs.

To discover your dog's threshold, it's easier if you have a friend or neighbour with a calm dog. Arrange to meet in a large open space, one where other dogs are sparse; if possible, you could hire a private field to ensure you are the only ones there.

Firstly, you and your dog go to the end of the field, having already arranged for your friend to enter once you have the distance between you. Now all you have to do is observe your dog as your friend's dog walks around gradually decreasing the distance between you.

You are looking for signs that your dog is starting to feel uncomfortable, by now you already know the obvious of barking/lunging etc but I want you to look at the small signs, the body language that comes before the barking and lunging. You would expect your dog to look, that's ok, but staring and leaning forward, raised tail (unless usual position) ears back or pushed forward towards the dog is a sign of starting to consider a negative reaction.

Here are a few simple illustrations of signs of anxiety and a dog likely to over react when put under pressure.

This dog is showing a raised tail position, whilst leaning slightly forward. His mouth is tight and is likely to be the warning signs of an aggressive reaction.

This dog is showing whale eye. Whale eye is a sign that a dog is really not comfortable with the situation.

One thing to notice in all three pictures is that the dog stares intently at whatever it is that is causing them to feel uncomfortable.

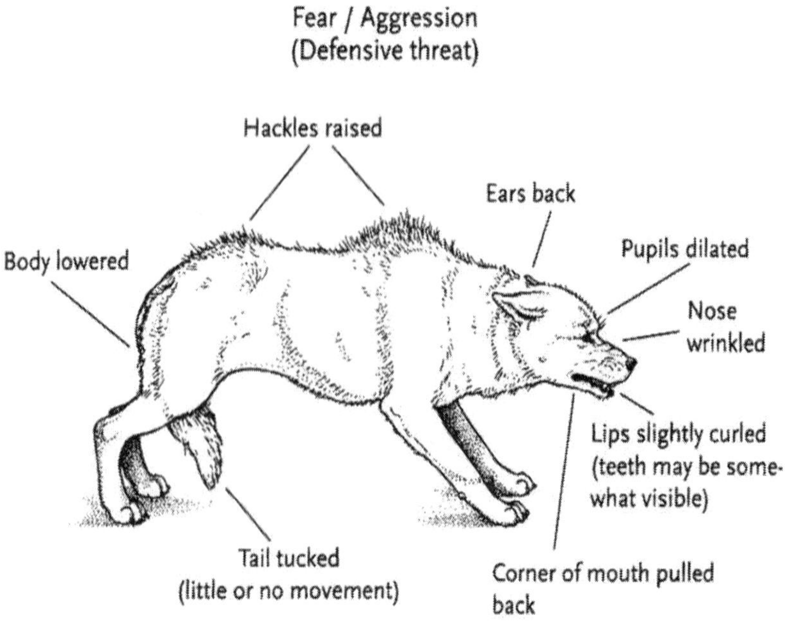

These images are from Bing.com, they can allow you to notice the body language many anxious overreactive dogs will display.

If you see any of these signs it is the point to ask the other owner/dog to stop moving forward and leave the field. You now have your baseline threshold, the distance that your dog can cope with seeing another dog.

The next step is to think about where you can now walk to enable you to see dogs but where you can keep the distance needed to stay below threshold. I know this can be difficult and unlikely walks will be perfect every day but finding open spaces to walk in is a must. We are at the stage in training where you need to bite the bullet and allow your dog to see dogs again, after all, how can you work on your dog’s emotions and behaviour by avoiding dogs altogether?

Think about driving to more suitable locations for your walks, particularly if you live in a very dog populated area.

Keeping walks short at this point and treating them like training sessions is what is required. If your dog has had a week off then you've already seen that short walks will be fine, allowing you to not get anxious about the fact that you've got to take the dog on long walks again! It is important that you and your dog keep as relaxed as possible.

You are nearly ready to get walking, just one more very important part of your training.

Good Associations

So now you know the point where your dog can cope with a dog in their eyeline, it's time to start changing how they feel. Changing how they feel when they see the other dogs will help them to make better choices.

At this point it's worth saying that your dog may never be skipping in a meadow with other dogs, the aim of this book is to make your walks much more relaxed and for your dog to cope with other dogs around him/her. I think it is important to have realistic ideas as to how far your dog can go in his/her development. For some, the end result may be that they can actually have canine friends, like my Jazz did, for others just being able to walk down the street and pass another dog is going to be the best they can do, but that's ok. After all, you got a dog to be your companion, to go walking with you, not to play with the other dogs in the park. We must remember to not put pressure on our dogs, let them be the best dog they can be, the most relaxed dog they can be and enjoy them.

We can start this process by associating something your dog likes with something that upsets them, in this case, another dog.

Firstly you need to prepare by chopping up lots of small high value treats and ensuring you have plenty in a readily accessible treat bag EVERY walk. Also make sure you have a favoured tuggy toy with you for those dogs who enjoy play.

Timing is very important in the process of changing how your dog feels. Your marker word is going to be your way of letting them know when he/she has shown the right behaviour when seeing a dog, and your dog already knows that he/she is going to be rewarded by something they like. This is the association, see a dog = get a tasty treat or have a game. With this happening EVERYTIME your dog sees a dog, your dog will start to look forward to seeing dogs and this is where their emotions toward the 'enemy' start to change.

Over the next few days or weeks, dependent on the dog, your dog may start to see a dog and look back at you. This is because he/she has started to associate the other dog with a reward, something he/she likes.
This is even better as, if they focus on you, then they can't be stressing about the other dog. When this starts to happen, hold off your marker word and treats until your dog looks at you, then mark and reward. Now your dog is being rewarded for making better choices.

Now where the timing is so important should be explained below:

- Your dog spots a dog – No reaction, just looks – you say 'yes' and give a tasty treat, your dog looks again (as the dog is still in sight) – no reaction, just looks – you say 'yes' and reward. Repeat until the other dog has disappeared.

- Your dog spots a dog – Reacts (possibly as too close) – No marker or reward (please note shortly you will read what to do if this happens)

You are probably wondering what to do if you miss the association training and your dog goes over threshold, starting to bark or lunge.

We need to make things clear to your dog, what's acceptable and good behaviour and what we don't want them to do. Contrary to some things you read online, I believe it is ok to tell your dog 'no' or 'leave' (leave training should be continuing from your first week). If we aren't clear with boundaries or let our dog know when he/she is behaving inappropriately then how are they supposed to learn from us? We are not just their owners, we are the people they should trust, listen to and learn from; you are all trainers of your own dogs.

So, on the occasions where timing is missed or your dog goes over threshold, you need to be clear, immediately say 'leave' and turn and walk away, giving your dog more distance so the escalation can decline more quickly and letting him/her know you did not like the behaviour they exhibited. Once you have created more space from the other dog and your dog has ceased the barking/lunging, you can turn back round and allow your dog to start again. This needs to be seen as a training opportunity, you can still reward for good behaviour with the same 'enemy' dog once you have created more distance and your dog is only looking. Start the association training again.

Avoiding dogs is never going to deal with your dog’s issues; try every day to at least see some dogs until your confidence grows. Equally, if you feel like some days you really aren't in the right mind set or you're having an off day where you know you won't do your best for your dog, then don't walk, hire a secure private field or go somewhere you know will be really quiet. None of us are perfect and your dog will benefit more from you being able to understand your own moods as well as theirs!

It's important this week to continue with your 'leave', 'wait' and 'look' training, all of these, as I said before, help with self-control and controlling your dog's behaviour. The more you do small training sessions at home, the more these commands become embedded in your dog's brain the more likely they are to listen. Keep referring back to Chapter 2 for the notes on these.

Also don't forget to play regularly with your dog at home and on walks, doing the training from Chapter 2.

Take this opportunity to take a breath and look back at what you have accomplished so far. If you have followed all the training so far, you should be seeing small changes, you will hopefully be seeing a more relaxed dog and I really hope your confidence has grown too, making you feel more relaxed and positive.

Jazz enjoying off lead time, relaxed and happy.

Chapter 4: Food motivation issues

If your dog is very food orientated then you may not need this chapter and can probably move on to Chapter 5 or, of course, you could just read it anyway!!

If you have a dog that doesn't see food as a top priority, the dog that can take it or leave it, then this chapter is for you.

I am going to use this chapter to explain how we can make food our friend, even with dogs who don't see treats as a priority, making your training go more smoothly.

To use food successfully we need the dog to see it as a reward; a reward is only a reward if the dog believes it is!

Switching to a method that means the dog has to earn his/her daily food allowance and ditching the bowl can really transform your training.

It is a fairly simple method, you just get rid of the bowl and put your dog's food allowance aside to be used throughout the day.

Most people worry that their dog doesn't eat all the food for the first couple of days, this is nothing to worry about. In order to get the dog motivated then you need them to get a little hungry and realise there are no free meals anymore, once they realise this then food becomes a much higher motivator.

Now that you have their food to hand, use it throughout the day in the house and on the walks as rewards, remember, if your dog doesn't listen or do what you were looking for or behave in the right way then he/she doesn't earn the food.

Don't be tempted to give them what’s left at the end of the day, if they haven't earnt it, they can't have it! Just trust that your dog won't starve himself, he will realise to pay attention when food is on offer!

Switching to this method does not necessarily mean you'll need to do it forever, but for the next couple of months whilst you are working on their behaviour and training it can be a game changer.

You can also improve the smell and taste of any kibble used by placing the food in a sandwich bag and adding a garlic clove, seal the bag and then marinade it overnight. The scent could make your kibble more appealing.

I will take this chapter to also discuss why I don't believe 'flooding' is an option with overreactive dogs.

Flooding is a term used to describe when you inundate a dog or person with something so, for example, if a person was terrified of spiders, do we think they could be cured by surrounding them with spiders?

Many clients have told me how their dog doesn't bark/lunge when there are lots of dogs about, this is not a sign that they are cured! The reason they don't react is because they can't focus on one dog when flooded, so the dog looks like its ok but in reality the dog is overwhelmed and so keeps quiet.

It is not a method I would choose to use with overreactive dogs.

Chapter 5: keep on training and self-control

At this point you should be two to three weeks into your training so I just want to remind you of your home training that should still be taking place.

Every day at home you should still be practicing and moving forward with the stages of the 'leave' (Chapter 2), the 'look' training should now be ready to move outside and practiced initially with minimal distraction, gradually increasing the distraction as you progress.

The 'look' (Chapter 2) is a useful command to allow you to get your dog's focus when passing something that you really don't want them to pay too much attention to, it is often a useful command to use alongside your lead walking, after all, they can't be focusing on other things and be looking at you.

The 'wait' (Chapter 2) is a very useful command as I said earlier, to teach self-control. But to really teach your dog to control his/her impulses better, you need to keep increasing the difficulty of your training. By now you should have a steady wait with some distance and a decent length of time. Those two areas of training are the easier part, it's now time to look at doing the wait during distractions.

At home, start with using yourself as the distraction; by this, I mean rather than standing still now start to move about. This could be turning on the spot in a circle, waving your arms or touching your toes. You can remind your dog to wait just before making these movements, after all, you are training not testing your dog, so you want to help them get it right as much as possible. Please remember at this point, always return to your dog to reward and release, don't call them to you, you are trying to create a solid wait where the dog believes not moving is the absolute best choice!
If your dog is doing well with these minor distractions then you can progress, the ideas are endless but here are a few to get you started:

- Remind your dog to wait and place food on the floor, then pick up the food, marker word and reward.

- Place a toy on the floor, pick it back up, return to the dog, release and play (you'll note that the release comes first if play is the reward, a dog can't play if still in the sit wait position

- Throw the toy, go pick it up, return to the dog, release and play

- Get someone else to enter the room, if the dog holds the wait, return to them, reward and release.

- Get someone to ring the doorbell, if the dog holds the wait, return, reward and release.

It is important to say that if your dog breaks the wait at any point during training, always correct them and get them to re position and start again. If you think you moved your dog forward too much, then just lessen the distraction and build up gradually. Training, not testing!

Hopefully you get the idea from this short list but as I said it is not exhaustive and I am sure you can come up with many more distractions to teach your dog to have self-control.

Whilst out on your training walks be sure to have a couple of play sessions, you and your dog engaging in fun is a must to continue to build that focus on you. You should know all the games by now from your week at home but, if needed, refer back to Chapter 2.

Continue with the association training. Depending on your dog, you may find you can now get slightly nearer to the 'enemy' whilst still keeping your dog calm; this means that your baseline threshold is getting better, your dog can cope nearer. This is obviously a great start but don't worry if you still have to stay the same distance away as you started, each dog is an individual and will improve at their own pace. This is not a race and you and your dog must work at your own pace, no rushing and absolutely no pressure.

We all know that other people and their dogs are unpredictable, we've all heard someone shouting out “it's ok he's friendly and just wants to play”, well this is every overreactive dog owners nightmare! And for you, the person who is trying to make your dog's life easier and your own, this attitude really doesn't help.

But equally it's something you can't control, so it's a good idea to get yourself and your dog out of there before the situation escalates. Teaching your dog a cue to mean, “we are going to turn away now and walk off at speed” and that this cue is a pleasant not panicked cue, can really help. It needs to be well practised when there is nothing going on.

You can start training it at home and then out on your walks when there are no dogs about. What you don't want is to teach it to be a cue to let your dog know a dog is coming!! It's simple to teach, just teach it well without distraction first!

Start by practising this when there are no distractions; this could be your garden or on quiet streets. Whilst walking forward, you will stop and start walking backwards a few paces, say ‘let’s go’ and encourage your dog to turn and walk towards you. Once your dog has turned, you can turn yourself and walk briskly off in the opposite direction together. Verbally and physically praise your dog.

This should be a positive move, not one done in panic or stress, just a change of direction. Be sure to keep your lead loose; this needs to become a cue for your dog to turn, not for you to physically move your dog with your lead, a tight lead will just increase the stress levels.

One other thing to talk about in relation to other people and their dogs when you are out walking. You must be prepared to defend your dog.

I want you to think about this scenario, you are walking down the street with your baby in a pram (now if you don't have kids, like me, you can still imagine this hopefully) and a complete stranger walks over and looks in the pram, he says, “what a beautiful baby” and we beam with pride, this is also seen as acceptable behaviour. However, should he say that and then proceed to scoop your baby in his arms and walk about, how long would it take you to stop this and protect your child? Remember this is a complete stranger that you know nothing about.

Now imagine it's your dog, your pride and joy, your companion. If an out of control dog (definition by law):

Your dog is considered dangerously out of control if it:

injures someone
makes someone worried that it might injure them

A court could also decide that your dog is dangerously out of control if either of the following apply:

it attacks someone's animal
the owner of an animal thinks they could be injured if they tried to stop your dog attacking their animal

is approaching and their owner is clearly not going to help, you will need to protect your dog as best you can, this could mean just getting away as soon as possible, it could mean stepping in front of your dog to block the other dog, it could just mean shouting to the other owner to get their dog asap.

Not only do we owe it to our dog to protect them but it also matters what they see you do. If you want your dog to trust you, to listen to you then don't leave him/her to look after themselves whilst restricted on a lead, if your dog can't trust you to protect him/her best you can then why would he/she listen to you when around the one thing that scares them?

Avoid parks where you know there are several out of control dogs often loose, avoid areas where the reputation is it's a free for all for dogs to play. These places are not right for your dog, be smart about where you walk. It is also for your sanity too, no one wants to come home from every walk stressed so much that they dread the next walk.

Do what you can to protect your dog and yourself.

Chapter 6: Making choices

I now want to cover some other exercises that you can do at home that help encourage your dog to make choices; our dogs are making choices all the time, the overreactive dog is choosing to bark and lunge for example. It is something that they have found works, at some point in their development or something that stems from their genetics, they felt pushed over their threshold most likely through fear. They most likely showed many signs and signals that the stress was getting too much but us humans are not the best at reading them and so they needed to speak louder, hence the barking and lunging behaviours I am sure you are aware of! When they made this choice and they found the other dog moved away or, more often than not, they were moved away, it meant that the overreactive dog realised how successful their choice had been, so it was repeated next time. It then most likely became a habit, not something they necessarily thought about but just knew it was their default behaviour to turn to.

With the training you are doing and have done, we now want them to see that they can make choices, better choices to behave in a different way.
So, there is some extra home training you can do to help the dog think more, work out things and basically make some choices that will be rewarding:

‘Mat training’

Place a towel or mat on the floor, wait to see what your dog does.

Be ready to mark and reward when your dog touches the mat, say ‘yes’ and then drop a treat onto the mat. Toss a treat away from the mat to encourage your dog to move away then wait and see what your dog does again. Repeat the mark and reward for every time your dog steps onto the mat, initially even if just one paw.

After several times of rewarding one paw, hold off the mark and treat until your dog has to think about offering more such as two paws or maybe even all of them.

Work through this over several sessions. Your next steps once the dog is going totally on the mat, hold off the mark and reward until your dog offers a sit or a lie down.

Basically, you are asking your dog to keep offering you behaviours, asking them to offer choices that allow you to reward them.

'Touch training'

How to teach it – Have treats ready in one hand with your fist closed. Offer the other hand out sideways, palm facing forward. The dog has to work out the rest! When he touches your hand with his nose, say 'yes' and reward with a treat from the other hand. Repeat this about 10 times at each practice session. When the dog doesn't touch your hand, just wait a few seconds before taking your hand away and starting again.

You must be patient, this is a free shaping exercise which means you can't help the dog, he must work it all out for himself.

Once the dog is doing this in repetition 10 times in a row, add the command "touch" and keep practising with the command. Eventually the dog will respond from a distance to the command.

Another important thing to do at this point is another threshold test (refer to Chapter 3), ideally with another calm dog. Can you see any improvement? Can your dog get nearer to the other dog? Does he just seem more relaxed and focused on you instead?

Not only can running another test at this point help you to see the improvements for your dog, but also for you. If you have followed all of the previous chapters and put in the work with your dog then you need a chance

to acknowledge your commitment to be a good dog owner! Give yourself a chance to review how you are doing and be proud of your dog and yourself.
Equally if you can only see small improvement, don't get disheartened, after all, how long has your dog been overreacting? It may be years or months and at this point you've potentially only done a few weeks training. Rome wasn't built in a day and training with dogs, when you are trying to change behaviour, is rarely an overnight fix! If it was, trainers would have way too much free time!

Time for a positive story!

At this point maybe you would like to hear of a story of a dog that I worked with called Vincent!
It started with an email from the owners with the subject being 'please help us'!

Vincent's new owners had only had him a few weeks from a rescue and very quickly discovered that whenever he saw a new person or dog he went straight into hysterical barking and growling.

They soon realised having visitors was a no go and walking him was an awful nightmare. But they didn't want to give up, they wanted to help him. Vincent was a Mini Schnauzer, only a couple of years old with not much of a history, so it was a case of starting from scratch.

We first met outside the training hall where I was working, I soon realised how badly the little chap was feeling, how terrified he was of everyone and every dog. For example, I couldn't get within 50 yards of Vincent without an explosion of barking and he made it very clear he would bite if given the chance.

He was lucky, his new owners wanted to help, they didn't want to give up on him. So, we began working together, following the training that has been discussed so far in this book both with dogs and people. I saw them for six weeks initially and then left them to continue the work and keep in touch.

When they rang several weeks later, they asked to meet me at a park local to them; well, to my joy he was so much better! We went for a walk and hardly any reaction at all which was amazing as the park we were in was very busy.

The fact that I could actually walk with him and at the end have a picture taken with him was fantastic.

Me, his owner Justyna and most importantly Vincent

I cannot explain how I felt that day. Was he perfect, no, but he was a normal little boy thanks to the dedication his owners showed.

As a trainer, you always want to know how everyone gets on and often we don't hear back, so to meet them again and see it for myself was amazing. The reason for telling this story is to give you that boost you may need at this point in your training.

Vincent was one of the worst cases I had seen of an overreactive dog and yet with the help he needed his walks became something far less stressful especially with people.

Chapter 7: Will socialisation help?

People often ask if 'socialisation' will help. This is something that cannot be answered simply with a yes because this is one subject a lot of people have different ideas about. Over socialisation causes as many problems as under socialisation!

With regards to your overreactive dogs there is certainly some 'social' walking that could be done. What I mean by this is that if you have family or friends with calm dogs then certainly walking with some distance between you can be a benefit. It is very important to walk in a quiet open space, keeping your dog under threshold as you walk. You will probably find that your dog relaxes a little after some time but don't be tempted to push the situation by allowing the dogs to get too close.

It is very important that you are sure the dog or dogs used are placid dogs, unlikely to react to your dog so that they will help benefit your dog rather than make things worse. Dogs observe other dogs and so using a calm dog that is giving off signals that he/she means no harm to your dog allows your dog to relax more. Be sure to continue your association training on these social walks.

I would suggest several walks with the same dog. If you

have success with seeing your dog relax more and seem to adjust to their new 'friend' then it would be ok to try another placid dog in the same way.

You will need to make judgements on this social walking, I would only start this part of the process once your dog can be comfortable with a reasonably small distance between you and other dogs. If your dog can only be 50 yards away then he clearly needs more time with the training until his threshold distance gets shorter.

During these walks make sure you continue your training; try not to get distracted with chatting where you are likely to miss any signals from your dog that he/she is becoming uncomfortable. If you really feel anxious about doing this then don't! You may feel that contacting a recommended, well respected trainer in your area for this may be of benefit.

Just a note on finding a trainer should you feel you would benefit, make sure you do your homework. Sadly, it is an industry that is not regulated. Look for recognised qualifications, experience and ask them about their methods, to ensure you are happy with the idea of them working with your dog and you.
If a trainer asks you to do anything that makes you uncomfortable or that you feel is detrimental to your dog, then stop.

Chapter 8: Can medication help?

This chapter is to discuss medication. Often people are reluctant to consider medication for dogs who have anxiety and stress, it seems to have a taboo element to it, however, we don't hesitate when our dog is sick to use medication.

There are plenty of natural products that state they can help ease anxiety levels, from Bach flower remedies to Adaptil collars/sprays. In my experience these can help some dogs but with others it will make no difference.

Then there are vet prescribed medications. These can have more of an effect, but again, it is the case of not everything works for every dog and your vet may have to try a few before having any effect on your dog.

The biggest question is not really if you should use them, at the end of the day, if they can help ease your dog's stress then why wouldn't you? It is more a question of does your dog really need them and taking the time to have a proper conversation with a behavioural vet. Behavioural vets have not only studied medicine but also behaviour and so, in my personal opinion, they would be the best people to visit to discuss your dog's anxiety and stress.
Like everything in life, research any natural products before buying them, an advert will always tell you they

are brilliant!!

If you really feel your dog could benefit from some help to allow you to train more effectively then please seek professional advice.

T touch is another therapy that I have seen have very positive effects on a dog’s anxiety. I will add a link at the end of the book as again, it is always best to speak to a qualified practitioner.

Chapter 9: The recall

By this stage you should be five to six weeks into your training and should be seeing some big changes in how your dog is feeling/reacting.

By now you should have a strong 'leave' command, a reliable 'look' command to gain focus, a steady ‘wait’, even with distractions, and be able to be nearer to dogs when out and about. You should have also learnt to enjoy play and interaction with your dog, increasing the strength of your relationship which in turn leaves you with a dog that listens to you even when other dogs are about.

At this stage I would start to work on the one thing we haven't tackled yet and that is the recall.

Now, don't panic, I am not suggesting that you will soon be letting your dog off in the park, in fact your dog's reactivity and possible aggression may mean that to be safe he/she may have to remain on lead, unless in a private secure area, for life. But even in a secure field or your garden, a decent response to recall is important.

There may be some of you reading this who hope to eventually be able to let your dog off, if you remember my girl Jazz who I spoke of in the introduction, she was able to go off lead and because her recall and leave were of a high level then I could control her off lead time even with the odd dog around.

It is a necessity, as explained in an earlier chapter, that a dog off lead has a recall so that he/she remains under control.

I always choose to teach a whistle recall; I find it more successful for several reasons. Firstly, everyone in the family sounds the same, a whistle never has a sore throat and a whistle never sounds annoyed!!

What follows is my whistle programme and information on how to use a longline:

Using a long line

When teaching a solid recall having control of your dog in public is a necessity! Have a look online at the law (dangerous dogs act and out of control dogs act). But as you get to the point of needing to practise recall out on walks with more distance a longer lead is needed.

Flexi leads can be very dangerous to both the dog and the human. The locks often break and then the dog is loose, if you grab the line as your dog runs it will burn through your skin (ouch) and in public areas your dog can easily tangle round people as you rush to reel your dog in!

A longline is more solid, doesn't rely on a lock and gives the dog a more 'off lead' feel. It is also easier to reel in and you can allow as long or short a lead as you wish. It is also thicker and so can be seen much better in public.

A longline attached to the collar is dangerous; if the dog runs at full pelt and hits the end of it ......imagine the yank you get in your arm, now imagine it attached to your neck..... not good! So, I would always recommend a harness for any longline training. This also helps with less tangling up!!

Don't just give the dog the full length, start with it at about 6ft long and then gradually give the dog more of it as you progress. With regards pulling, you still don't have to be dragged! Every time the dog reaches the end and starts to pull, stand still until the dog slackens the line and then move on again, repeat, repeat..... The longline gives them more freedom, however, that doesn't mean you have to allow pulling so start as you mean to go on. As you progress with the recall training it will allow you to work on distance and allow more room for playing. It will also allow you to improve your control positions (more about that in the coming weeks).

When your dog ignores your ONE recall cue, use the longline to bring the dog to you by reeling it in, not yanking. The dog does not get a reward for this obviously, but you have prevented it from just ignoring you showing the dog there is a consequence to ignoring you.

Week 1 of recall

This stage is to prepare the dogs for their basic recall training.

Your dog may have already learned bad habits, to ignore previous recall commands so it’s important that you follow this stage to make the new whistle signal have the wow factor!

During the whistle training I will refer to treats as bonus and simple. Bonus treats are high value, such as cheese, cooked chicken, sausages or anything else that your dog sees as amazing! Simple treats means kibble or lower value plain treats, something that your dog likes but not as much as the bonus treats.

During the whistle training you will also need to use verbal and physical praise as we eventually want to get to the point where treats are rarely used and so it is important that we still let the dog know they did well!

Level 1 – Have a plate of bonus treats. Put one in your hand with your fist closed. Get the dog interested in your hand with the food in, give your signal (pip, pip) and then open your hand and feed the dog. Immediately feed your dog another two chunks of bonus rewards. You want to make this first introduction to the whistle an amazing one! Repeat this exercise over the next three days, a couple of times a day. Also, this week when you feed your dog, give the same two pips as you put their bowl down.

Level 2 – Over the following few days repeat Level 1 but this time mix up the treat value from bonus to simple, so that the dog does not know which treat it will get. Be sure to always give a treat though.

You have now associated the sound of the whistle with treats/food and big praise from yourself. Bear in mind the dog is, at this point, only doing this at home with no distractions. The whistle should not be being used at any other time or location at this point.

Week 2 of recall

Your dog has already learned that the whistle is associated with food; during these next stages you will get the dog to see that the sound has a meaning. It's important that this training is done at home with no distractions. To get a decent recall outside, you need a reliable recall at home.

Level 1 - Have your treats on you or on a plate up high. With your dog in the same room not doing anything such as chewing or playing, busy yourself so that your dog is a couple of feet away from you. Turn to your dog and use the whistle, as your dog comes to you say 'yes' and reward with a bonus treat. Repeat this five times throughout the day in the same room but, if you can, increase the distance.

If your dog ignores the whistle, DO NOT repeat the whistle, just get down and make yourself interesting to the dog.

Repeat the exercise on the second day but this time using simple treats for four of the recalls and bonus treat for one of the recalls.

Day three repeat with three recalls done with basic treats and two recalls without any treats just a big fuss, both verbal and physical.

IF you have any failed recalls you may need to do bonus treat recalls for a few more days until you can complete this stage with 100% success at each level.

Moving rooms – Repeat all of the above in a new room in the house, starting back with the bonus treats and then working your way through the above training schedule.

Again, if all successful you can move on to the next stage.

Recall from one room to another – When the dog is in one room, make your way to another room and whistle. Initially use bonus treats again to begin with for the first five recalls, then move to simple treats and then do some without moving. Don't make it a pattern as you start to remove the food, for example it might be 1st recall basic treat, 2nd no treat, 3rd basic treat, 4th premium treat, 5th no treat..... practice this until you get 100% recalls over several days.

Recalling from things the dog wants is an important lesson for the dog to learn.

Over the next few days, you want to start reducing treats until you get to only giving food one in three or four recalls. Remember not to have a pattern that the dog can work out! Sometimes bonus treats, sometimes simple, sometimes big fuss. Over these few days, practice all the recalls you have done so far so same room, room to room and from food.

Garden Time – Time to take the recall outside. Using your own garden, over the next few days carry out recalls in your garden, gradually increasing the distance. Start with premium treats, then basic treats then a ratio of treats and no treats as before. Practice until you have 100% recall ….remember, never repeat the whistle command more than once.

IF this has all gone successfully then you now have a basic recall ...well done. Your recall is now, however, only trained at home so in order to move on you need to be able to answer yes to these questions....

1/ Can you recall from room to room in your house?
2/ Can you recall your dog in the garden?
3/ Does your dog come quickly when you call?
4/ Have you faded the treats down to one in four recalls?

If yes to all of the above then you are ready to move onto the next stage.

Week 3 of recall

So, we are now into Week 3 of the training. All your basic training has been done hopefully! And you have practised hard hopefully! It's time to start working with distraction.

When you first start increasing these distractions make sure you start with bonus treats, only moving to basic treats and no treats after you have had 100% response from your dog.

Remember you are trying to build a permanent reliable recall....this doesn't happen overnight. Below is a list of recalls to practice this week; a longline should still be being used if the dog cannot be 'trusted' off lead. You are aiming for success not failure!!!

1/ New locations – parks, woods etc on lead
2/ Recall from greeting family members in the house
3/ Recall from visitors to the house
4/ Recall from seeing a dog in the distance – not a dog that is right in your dog's face, on lead
5/ Recall from sniffing a bush/tree/lamppost
6/ Recall from food
7/ Recall from seeing joggers/bikes/skateboards
8/ Recall in the garden when playing with someone else or themselves
9/ Recall in garden when just running around excited (like dogs do!)

ALWAYS a big fuss and verbal reward as soon as they start coming. Be exciting and pleased with your dog. Practise every day and remember **DO NOT** repeat the recall cue, always only use it once.

Week 4 of recall

So far you have trained a really solid recall in the home and garden and also proofed this with people hopefully! However, most of us aren't too worried about recall at home, we want it out on walks!

Firstly, you need to make a list of walks that you are going to use to practise your recalls. In each location you will:

- **Avoid unnecessary distractions**
- **Interact with your dog**
- **Set up recall practices**
- **Practise practise practise!**

Moving to a new place to train is distraction enough so you don't want football games, joggers, lots of other dog walkers, hundreds of rabbits, bikes etc. You can avoid these by maybe walking at unsociable hours, when it’s raining or just find rural locations that are quiet. Take with you lots of bonus treats, simple treats and your whistle plus a toy.

When your dog is off lead on the walk, keep your whistle in your mouth and anytime your dog starts running back to you by himself, whistle, to again enforce your command and reward. In between recall practises, interact with your dog by either playing with him/her or maybe scent games so your dog sees you as fun and doesn't learn to just run off to find his own fun!

Have a 'zone' around you that you decide is how far your dog can go away from you. The further you allow your dog to run away from you the harder the recall will be. Do other training at each location too, like sits/downs/waits and every now and again put your dog back on lead and do some lead walking practise. Putting the dog back on lead means you can have a break from watching what your dog is up to and allow you to move around the location and practise in different areas.

As before you will need to reduce the reward to the simple treats and when you feel ready reduce to some recalls with no treats but always a big fuss and interaction. Every now and again give the dog a 'jackpot' where he gets lots of treats for doing a recall. Remember we want the dog to never know what he's getting!

Chapter 10: My final thoughts

By now I am hoping you are really pleased with your progress but I feel I do need to suggest what to do if you feel you are not getting anywhere or if you feel overwhelmed. As with everything in life, not all training will work for every dog and we always have to be ready to look for adjustments to make or ask for more help.

Firstly, consider going back a few weeks, maybe you can see a place in the training where things started to go wrong, maybe you can remember an incident that set your dog back or yourself or maybe you can admit that you moved too far too quickly or indeed that you haven't done as much work as needed? Any of these reasons are more than possible and nothing to beat yourself up about! You can always start again if really needed, maybe when you have more time or are in a better place in yourself to start.

Of course, contacting a trainer to help is another way to move even further forward with your training as discussed before. I am not precious enough to think that this book can help everyone! I appreciate that many people will want the support a trainer can give in person and anyone reading this in Kent is more than welcome to contact me personally.

Also please remember that your training shouldn't end here, after all, at this point it's likely only been six to eight weeks, continue to work with your dog and enjoy watching them improve until your walks are once again something to look forward to. Your dog has potentially been overreacting for months or years so you cannot expect six weeks to be enough.

When we commit to a dog we are committing to guiding him/her for his/her entire life, so don’t give up!

I also feel the need to address one more thing in this book, something that can often be seen causing contention amongst trainers and owners alike, and that is the subject of aversives.

Aversives, or consequences as they are often called, is anything that is used to create a negative consequence when a dog displays a behaviour that we don't want. The reason it is a much-argued debate on places such as Facebook or amongst trainers is because many people believe dogs should only be trained using positive methods, that dogs shouldn't even be told no and then many other trainers believe that sometimes balance is needed between reward and consequence. Often people see aversives as being pain related; this is often not true but of course it does depend on the person using it and the dog.

I have a few opinions on it myself that I will share with you. Firstly, I would never say never to considering using different methods of training depending on what the situation was. Let me give you an example, if something that a dog was doing was potentially going to cost him his life but could be fixed using a consequence, would I use it correctly? Yes, I would. But would I assess the dog thoroughly and use the mildest consequence possible, yes, I would.

If we think about life, every species has things happen

to them that are aversive, including us. Picture a puppy raiding a bin, that bin is metal and is situated on a tiled hard floor. The puppy jumps up at the bin as it can smell food, the bin falls and crashes to the floor causing a loud sound, the dog is scared off and moves away. Due to this unpleasant consequence there is a strong possibility that puppy will stay away from the bin. I doubt that the puppy will be scarred for life, he will most likely just get over it and move on with his next adventure having learned that bins really aren't worth the effort! (Thank you to Sandra for this great analogy).

Is it my first choice of training, no, if I can and it improves the dog's behaviour, I would 100% prefer to use reward based training, but to close my mind to other methods that could keep that dog out of rescue, to keep that dog alive and keep that dog safe and happy is in itself a negative response and failure as a trainer, in my opinion. Having many 'tools' in your toolbox or many methods in your mind is what makes good trainers good!

The reality is not all 'bad' behaviours can be got rid of by just ignoring it, in fact this can be downright dangerous.

I do believe, however, that if an aversive is being used it should never be attempted without a professional showing you the correct way. They are like anything;

they must be used appropriately to be effective and when used incorrectly they can do much more harm than good. So please don't buy tools that are advertised as quick fixes, such as anti bark collars. They really aren't, speak with a professional instead.

I truly hope by now that you are pleased with your progress, that your dog is happier because that is the only reason for writing this book. I would love to see less dogs in rescue due to reactivity issues, less dogs euthanised due to being perceived as 'aggressive' dogs and more owners prepared to help their dogs along their journey. If you are seeing progression and feeling more confident then, well done, keep up your training and remember, you are your dog’s protector and he/she deserves the best.

I think this is a great analogy for dog training, it is so much easier to make progress with small steps.

I couldn't finish this book without mentioning my last dog Alfie, another troubled soul with a tenacious nature. Recently he left me but I will always be grateful for all that he taught me and how much he showed me that a dog could change with a truly understanding relationship with me, his pal.
You'll never be forgotten.

Testimonials from past clients and colleagues:

"Jordi, Rudi and I first met Alexis at dog training club, the second club we tried as we didn't feel the first one was suitable. It soon became clear that, along with all the relevant 'formal' qualifications, Alexis is one of those trainers that possesses a unique 'natural' ability and love for helping dogs and owners. Whilst primarily there for training pup Rudi (as Jordi was an 'older' dog), watching and listening to her lessons helped me immensely with Jordi, who was an anxious, fearful dog that did not always cope with new situations. Fast forward 10 years or so and Miss Scully came along. Whilst I was prepared for her it was a shock to the system to arrive at a class with a dog that would actually prefer anything and everyone else rather than me! With Alexis' training, we slowly but surely managed to turn things around, at times it seemed like we took one step forward and two steps back, it would have been easier (for me) to give up, but with Alexis' help we got there!!!!

Alexis explains things in plain English so that us owners can understand, and through her training gives us the skills to work out how and why certain behaviours are happening, and, more importantly how to cope and change dogs' and owners' outlooks. There are no 'miracle' cures in dog training, be prepared to follow the instructions she gives, don't skip steps and you will get there, just like us!"

Linda - Buttonpushers Limited

"Clear sensible training from a lady dedicated to improving the welfare of all animals. Alexis has been, and will continue to be, an enormous help to me and my reactive dog."

Anne and Tango

"I first met Alexis when my dog Sasha was just 15 weeks old at puppy training classes. Sasha was very nervous of people and dogs, the whole world really. Even though initially I felt out of my depth, Alexis helped us so much with our journey for the better and continues to be part of our journey to this day almost seven years on. Thanks to her skills and mentoring, and teaching me what I needed to know to help my dog, I now have a completely different outlook. Sasha is more confident and calm, she rarely reacts and she knows to look to me if we run into any issues when out. Through real life situations and controlled socialisation we had both been taught by Alexis how to handle each different scenario creating a much more relaxed dog who is a pleasure to walk and have in my life.

We are truly thankful to have met Alexis all those years ago and know if we do end up needing additional help she is still there to this day for support. It really does help when your trainer is someone so passionate and open to learning new skills about what they can do to be able to help dogs and their humans that really do need guidance to improve their relationship with their dogs and the skills to keep their dogs' lives happy and full of enrichment."

Jenna Hodgkins and Sasha

"I first met Alexis when I attended obedience classes with my dog who had selective hearing! I was so impressed with her training methods I went on to help in classes - I loved seeing the change from that first day - most knowing hardly any commands to the finished results on assessment day - the look on the owners faces said it all - the training had worked."

Sue Archer and Barney, sadly departed but a wonderful dog to have at training.

"I have worked with Alexis in classes for 5 years during which time I learned an enormous amount from her. Not least of all about over reactivity in dogs. Those classes were my favourites, watching the dogs change from unhappy, over stimulated dogs to more confident happy dogs and their owners relax and enjoy their dogs and their interactions with other dogs and humans. The humans knowing they then had the tools to cope with situations and do the right thing for their dogs and the dogs having learned how to calm down, listen and enjoy interaction. I also have many more tools in my own dog training box for my own dogs both now and in the future."

Bina Martin and her dogs Stan and Poppy, often used as stooges in class.

"Working in rescue I have experienced dogs with all sorts of issues and problems. Reaching out to Alexis has helped me progress myself and my ability to train but also understand what each dog needs as an individual. Alexis opened my mind to the aspect of the dogs and their feelings and the environmental factors that effects every dog some way or another. I am lucky enough to call her a colleague and also a friend and the dogs that find their way into our care are understood and engaged with correctly thanks to Alexis"

Lisa McConvey, animal rescuer.

"Alexis helped us with our young rescue miniature schnauzer, Vincent, when it became clear after adoption that he was extremely reactive towards both humans and dogs. Whilst he was in kennels he had not displayed any signs of his problems. His reactivity was so bad that he wasn't able to join any group activities at all, but Alexis and her team took the time to work one to one with us. After a few weeks, we started to see he was getting more settled with people and since then we have managed to safely introduce strangers to him. Now, after initial hesitation, visitors are usually accepted quickly and on walks they are rarely a problem for him. Whilst it is still an ongoing battle with other dogs, Alexis started us off with the right training foundations and confidence to continue to help Vincent with his issues".

Craig, Justyna and Vincent

Useful links and websites :

www.dog-games-shop.co.uk/perfect-fit-fleece-dog-harness.html

This is the Perfect fit harness recommended in the book.

www.gencon-allin1.co.uk

This is the head collar that I prefer over all other makes.

www.companyofanimals.co.uk/brand-product/halti-training-lead-2/

The training lead with 2 clips, perfect to use with the perfect fit harness.

www.doggiesolutions.co.uk

The muzzle I have advised in the book.

www.pdti.org

The pet dog training instructors group that I am a member of. You can find a trainer on their website.

www.kentcompaniondogtraining.co.uk
@Alexiskcdt

My website and Facebook page.

www.ttouch.com

T touch therapy website

Printed in Great Britain
by Amazon

67817687R00059